Japanese Kanji for JLPT N5

Master the Japanese Language Proficiency Test N5

Clay and Yumi Boutwell

Copyright © 2018-2024 Kotoba Books
www.TheJapanShop.com/bundles
www.TheJapanesePage.com
www.MakotoPlus.com

All rights reserved.

KANJI—an Introduction

Hiragana, katakana, and kanji are the cornerstones of the Japanese writing system. Originally imported from China centuries ago, kanji characters have undergone significant evolution in Japan, diverging markedly from their original forms. Although the pronunciation of many kanji differs from their Chinese counterparts, understanding Japanese kanji can often provide clues to the meanings of written Chinese, even for those with no formal study of the language.

In Japan, literacy requires knowledge of approximately two thousand kanji. However, learning just a few hundred kanji allows readers to navigate most texts, with occasional support from a dictionary. This book focuses on these essential characters, offering you the foundation needed to begin your journey toward kanji mastery—a challenging yet rewarding endeavor.

Who is this for?

This guide is designed for beginners who are already familiar with hiragana. We have deliberately excluded romaji to encourage authentic learning of Japanese script. If you need to familiarize yourself with hiragana or require a refresher, we recommend our companion volume, "Hiragana: The Basics of Japanese."

About JLPT Kanji

The organizers of the Japanese Language Proficiency Test (JLPT) no longer release an official list of kanji required for the exam. However, they have indicated that the N5 level includes 103 kanji. This book covers the 81 kanji that were previously necessary for the old JLPT 4 test, which is considered equivalent to the current N5 level. Additionally, we have included twenty-two more kanji that appear frequently on official practice tests or are fundamental for beginners to learn.

While it's not possible to guarantee that all these kanji are designated "N5" kanji, we can affirm that most of them are typically encountered at this level and are crucial for early learning.

On / Kun Readings

Each kanji typically has a core meaning—be it an abstract concept or a tangible object—and two primary sets of pronunciations: 音読み *on yomi* and 訓読み *kun yomi*. On yomi is based on the original Chinese pronunciation, adapted by the Japanese, while kun yomi uses native Japanese words corresponding to the kanji's meaning.

Over time, changes in pronunciation have led some kanji to acquire several different readings, which we illustrate with numerous example words throughout this book.

Effective Kanji Study Strategies

Success with kanji requires a positive attitude from the start. Without a passion for these characters, it's easy to become overwhelmed given their complexity and multitude.

Here are our top tips for effective kanji learning:

- **Kanji Parts**: Focus on the radicals, or basic components, of kanji to help recognize and remember more intricate characters.
- **Use Spaced Repetition**: Implement tools like Anki (https://apps.ankiweb.net/) that utilize spaced repetition algorithms to enhance memory retention.
- **Contextual Learning**: Study kanji within the context of words and sentences, which aids in grasping both meanings and pronunciations. Learn kanji while you learn vocabulary.
- **Visual Mnemonics**: Employ mnemonic techniques to associate abstract kanji with memorable visuals or stories.
- **Consistent Practice**: Set aside regular study time each day for kanji practice to ensure long-term retention.
- **Engage with Real Materials**: Read materials such as manga, newspapers, and books in Japanese to see kanji used in real-life contexts.
- **Set Manageable Goals**: Learn a small number of new kanji daily to prevent burnout and encourage steady progress.
- **Practice Reading Aloud**: This reinforces the pronunciations of kanji.

- **Seek Feedback**: Obtain input from native speakers or teachers to correct mistakes and clarify doubts. Feel free to reach out to us with questions at help@thejapanshop.com.

Kanji Stroke Order

Learning the correct stroke order is important because:

- It ensures your kanji look authentic and are easily recognizable.
- It aids in memorizing new kanji.
- Kanji dictionaries often organize characters by stroke count.
- Proper stroke order reflects respect for kanji as an art form, noticeable by those well-versed in Japanese.

See the next page for general rules for stroke order. Even if you do not plan on regularly writing kanji by hand—a practice that has become less essential in the digital age—it is still beneficial to familiarize yourself with the correct stroke order.

Are you ready to accept the challenge?

Clay & Yumi Boutwell
help@thejapanshop.com

http://www.TheJapanShop.com/bundles
https://www.MakotoPlus.com

Kanji Stroke Order Cheat Sheet

**START FROM THE TOP-LEFT OF THE KANJI AND
WORK DOWN TO THE BOTTOM-RIGHT.**

RULE #1 : From top to bottom

三 (the number three)

言 (to say)

RULE #2 : From left to right

州 (a (U.S. state)

And when you have both a vertical and horizontal
go horizontal first.

十 (the number ten)

But it wouldn't be fun without exceptions!

田 (rice field) 丨 冂 冂 闬 田

王 (king) 一 丅 王 王

RULE #3 : If you have left, right, and center options, work from the center.

水 (water) 亅 汀 氺 水

糸 (thread) 〻 糸 糸 糸 糸 糸

RULE #4 : If there is an outside shape surrounding an inside one, **the outside comes first.**

国 (country) 丨 冂 冂 国 国

風 (wind)　ノ 几 冋 風

Except when the outside is shaped like a "C"

区 (district)　一 フ メ 区

RULE #5 : If there is a vertical line going through other parts, it comes last *or at least later.*

中 (inside, middle)　丨 冂 口 中

書 (write, writing)　ㄱ ㅋ ㅋ 聿 書

And if there is a horizontal line that overlaps other parts, it goes last.

女 (woman)　く 女 女

RULE #6 : If there is an "X" or a crossing of diagonals the top-right to bottom-left goes first.

文 (literature)

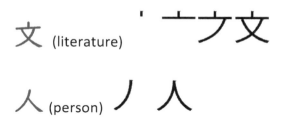

人 (person)

RULE #7 : If there is a ⻌, it goes last:

進 (proceed)

Table of Contents

Subscribe Today

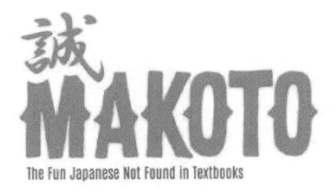

EVERY MONTH AUTOMATICALLY

www.MakotoPlus.com

**Download the Latest Makoto Issue | Weekly Lessons |
Podcast Bonus Content | Reusable TheJapanShop.com
Coupon | Monthly Freebies**

かんじ
漢字

N5

さあ、
はじめましょう

Chapter One: Kanji 1-10

And so begins your kanji journey and it couldn't get any easier! (...and believe me it won't!)

JLPT N5: 1 / 103 | 1 Stroke

On: イチ
Kun: ひと・つ

Meaning: one; 1

It is a number "1" on its side. Draw the single stroke from left to right.

Examples:

<ruby>一<rt>いち</rt></ruby> one; the number one

<ruby>一<rt>いちばん</rt></ruby>番 #1; the best

世界<ruby>一<rt>せかいいち</rt></ruby> the best in the world

<ruby>一<rt>ひとり</rt></ruby>人 one person; alone

どこが<ruby>一番<rt>いちばん</rt></ruby>いいところですか？

Where is the best place?

JLPT N5: 2 / 103 | 2 Strokes

Two lines = two, logical!

On: 二
Kun: ふた・つ

Meaning: two; 2

Two lines make Two!

Stroke Order:

Examples:

に
二 two

だいに
第二 the second

にがつ
二月 February [the 2nd month]

フロリダの１２月は暑いですか？
じゅうにがつ あつ

Is Florida hot in December?

[Foreign (non-Japan) place names and foreigner names are written in katakana unless there is a kanji for the name.]

JLPT N5: 3 / 103 | 3 Strokes

Three lines = 3

On: サン
Kun: みっ・つ

Meaning: three

From top to bottom. Remember, the middle is shorter.

Stroke Order:

Examples:

さん
三 three

さんかく
三角 triangle

さんがつ
三月 March [the 3rd month]

さんがつ　にほん　い
三月に日本に行きます。

I'm going to Japan in March.

[The months are easy: a number from 1-12 + がつ]

JLPT N5: 4 / 103 | 5 Strokes

Think of two little legs dangling in a FOUR sided box.

On: シ
Kun: よん; よっ・つ

Meaning: four

Stroke Order:

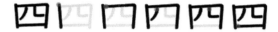

Examples:

四 four [both し and よん pronunciations mean "four" but they are used in different contexts.]

四級 4th class; 4th level (of an exam)

四月 April [the 4th month]

四匹の猫を飼っています。

I have four cats.

[The verb for owning/having pets is 飼う *kau*—not to be confused with the verb "to buy" which is 買う *kau*.]

JLPT N5: 5 / 103 | 4 Strokes

五 is an artist's impression of the number 5.

On: ゴ

Kun: いつ・つ

Meaning: five

Stroke Order:

五 五 丁 五 五

Examples:

ご
五 five

ごがつ
五月 May [the 5th month]

ご かげつ
五ヶ月 (a span of) five months [So far we have seen that adding a number between 1-12 with がつ makes the month names. But here is how to say a duration of months: # + か + げつ—notice it is "げつ" not "がつ"; the small ケ in ケ月 is pronounced "ka" and not "ke" as you might think; it is a counter for months]

十五まで数えます。

じゅうご　かぞ

I can count to fifteen.

JLPT N5: 6 / 103 | 4 Strokes

A picture of a man stretching his hands and legs is the character for "6."

On: ロク
Kun: むっ・つ

Meaning: six

Stroke Order: Make sure the legs do not touch the top.

Examples:

<ruby>六<rt>ろく</rt></ruby> six

<ruby>六日<rt>むいか</rt></ruby> the 6th of the month

<ruby>六月<rt>ろくがつ</rt></ruby> June [the 6th month]

<ruby>六個<rt>ろっこ</rt></ruby>ほしいです。

I want six of them.

[ろく becomes ろっ before certain sounds.]

JLPT N5: 7 / 103 | 2 Strokes

A diagonal line through a "L" means "7."

On: シチ
Kun: なな・つ

Meaning: seven

Stroke Order: Start with the (almost) horizontal line.

七 一 七

Examples:

しち
七 seven

なな ふ し ぎ
七不思議 the Seven Wonders

しちがつ
七 月 July [the 7th month]

こんばん 「 しちにん さむらい
今晩、「七人の 侍 」をみます。

I will watch "Seven Samurai" tonight.

[Seven Samurai is a famous movie by Kurosawa Akira.]

JLPT N5: 8 / 103 | 2 Strokes

If you have studied katakana, you will notice this looks like "ハ *ha*." So *HAchi* = 8

On: ハチ
Kun: やっ・つ

Meaning: eight

Don't confuse this with 人 (person).

Stroke Order:

Examples:

<ruby>はち<rt></rt></ruby>
八 eight

<ruby>はちねんかん<rt></rt></ruby>
八年間 eight years time; a span of eight years

<ruby>はちがつ<rt></rt></ruby>
八月 August [the 8th month]

こんげつ　にじゅうはちにち　わたし　たんじょうび
今月の二十八日は 私 の誕生日です。

The 28th of this month is my birthday.

JLPT N5: 9 / 103 | 2 Strokes

Don't confuse this one with 力 (power)

On: キュウ; ク

Kun: ここの・つ

Meaning: nine

Stroke Order: Don't forget to make the hook at the end.

九 九 九

Examples:

きゅう
九　nine

きゅうかげつ
九 カ月　nine months

くがつ
九月　September [the 9th month]

こんげつ　くがつ
今月は九月です。

This month is September.

JLPT N5: 10 / 103 | 2 Strokes

5 + 5 = 十

On: ジュウ
Kun: と; とう

Meaning: ten

Start with the horizontal line.

Stroke Order:

Examples:

じゅうく
十九 19 [lit. 10 and 9]

きゅうじゅう
九十 90 [lit. 9 and 10]

じゅうにがつ
十二月 December [the 12th month]

わたしは十九歳です。
じゅうきゅうさい

I am nineteen.

Chapter Two: Kanji 11-20

One hundred has a one (━) at top.
JLPT N5: 11 / 103 | 6 Strokes

On: ヒャク
Kun:

Meaning: hundred

Stroke Order:

Examples:

<ruby>二<rt>に</rt></ruby><ruby>百<rt>ひゃく</rt></ruby> 200

<ruby>三<rt>さん</rt></ruby><ruby>百<rt>びゃく</rt></ruby> 300 [note: sound changes to a harder "b" sound]

ええと、<ruby>百<rt>ひゃく</rt></ruby><ruby>人<rt>にん</rt></ruby>くらい<ruby>来<rt>き</rt></ruby>ました。

Let's see... About a hundred people came.

[ええと is often used in spoken Japanese similar to

"umm."]

JLPT N5: 12 / 103 | 3 Strokes

It looks like a 10 [十] with a slanted line over it. Think of
the line as adding two extra 0's: 1000

千

On: セン
Kun: ち

Meaning: thousand

Stroke Order:

千 千 千 千

Examples:

せんえん
千円 1000 yen [yen is pronounced えん]

さんぜんにひゃく
三千二百 3,200

にせんねん
二千年 the year 2000

ごせんえん　　　　か
これは、五千円ほどで買えます。

This can be bought for about 5,000 yen.

JLPT N5: 13 / 103 | 3 Strokes

The next in numbers. Just add another 0.

万

On: バン; マン
Kun:

Meaning: ten thousand

Stroke Order: The stroke order for kanji like this is a little different. Start at the top horizontal line. The second stroke is the rightmost one that looks like フ.

万 万 万 万

Examples:

ひゃくまん
百 万　a million (1,000,000) [100 and 10,000]

いちまんえん
一 万 円　10,000 yen (about $100 USD)

ばんざい
万 歳　hurrah! banzai! hooray! [Usually said three times in a row while celebrating.]

いちまんえん
はい、一万円ぐらいあります。

Yes, I have about 10,000 yen.

JLPT N5: 14 / 103 | 4 Strokes

It looks like a father tying his tie.

On: フ
Kun: ちち; とう

Meaning: father

Stroke Order:

Examples:

お父さん a father
^{とう}

父の日 Father's Day
^{ちち ひ}

仕事が終わったら、お父さんはテレビの前で
ごろごろします。

After work, dad loafs around in front of the TV.

JLPT N5: 15 / 103 | 5 Strokes

Think of a **mother** holding two babies close to her.

On: ボ
Kun: はは; かあ

Meaning: mother

Stroke Order:

母 ㄴ 口 母 母 母

Examples:

お<ruby>母<rt>かあ</rt></ruby>さん a mother; mommy

<ruby>母<rt>はは</rt></ruby>の<ruby>日<rt>ひ</rt></ruby> Mother's Day

<ruby>保母<rt>ほ ぼ</rt></ruby> a kindergarten teacher; a nurse

あの<ruby>子<rt>こ</rt></ruby>はお<ruby>母<rt>かあ</rt></ruby>さんにいつもべたべたしています。

That child is always clinging to his mother.

JLPT N5: 16 / 103 | 4 Strokes

A picture of a friend giving another friend a hand.

友

On: ユウ
Kun: とも

Meaning: friend

This kanji is often used with words dealing with friendship or friendliness.

Stroke Order:

友 一 ナ 方 友

Examples:

<ruby>友<rt>とも</rt></ruby><ruby>達<rt>だち</rt></ruby> friends; a friend

<ruby>友<rt>ゆう</rt></ruby><ruby>情<rt>じょう</rt></ruby> friendship

<ruby>友<rt>ゆう</rt></ruby><ruby>好<rt>こう</rt></ruby><ruby>国<rt>こく</rt></ruby> a friendly nation

<ruby>途<rt>と</rt></ruby><ruby>中<rt>ちゅう</rt></ruby>で<ruby>友<rt>とも</rt></ruby><ruby>達<rt>だち</rt></ruby>に<ruby>会<rt>あ</rt></ruby>いました。

On the way, I ran into a friend.

JLPT N5: 17 / 103 | 3 Strokes

Think of a woman dancing.

女

On: ジョ

Kun: おんな

Meaning: woman; female

A female ninja is called *kunoichi*. If you combine hiragana *ku* く, katakana *no* ノ, and the kanji *ichi* 一 you get 女.

Stroke Order:

女 く 女 女

Examples:

かのじょ
彼女 1) her; 2) girlfriend

おんな　こ
女 の子 a girl

じょゆう
女優 an actress

かれ　おんな
彼は 女 をナンパばかりする。

He is always hitting on women.

JLPT N5: 18 / 103 | 7 Strokes

On: ダン
Kun: おとこ

Meaning: man; male

The top part 田 means "rice field" and 力 means "power." So a **powerful man** works in the **rice field**.

Stroke Order:

男 男 男 男 男 男 男 男

Examples:

だんじょ
男 女　men and women

おとこ
男 らしい　manly; like a man

ゆきおとこ
雪 男　the abominable snowman

あか　　　　　おとこ　　こ
赤ちゃんは 男 の子です。

The baby is a boy.

JLPT N5: 19 / 103 | 2 Strokes

This is a **person** with no head or arms doing a split.

On: ジン; ニン
Kun: ひと

Meaning: person; people

Stroke Order:

Examples:

<ruby>日<rt>に</rt>本<rt>ほん</rt>人<rt>じん</rt></ruby> a Japanese person

<ruby>大<rt>お</rt>人<rt>とな</rt></ruby> adult; a grown-up [irregular reading]

<ruby>外<rt>がい</rt>国<rt>こく</rt>人<rt>じん</rt></ruby> foreigner

<ruby>美<rt>び</rt>人<rt>じん</rt></ruby> a beautiful woman

<ruby>宇<rt>う</rt>宙<rt>ちゅう</rt>人<rt>じん</rt></ruby> a space alien

あなたは<ruby>美<rt>び</rt>人<rt>じん</rt></ruby>です。

You are a beautiful woman.

JLPT N5: 20 / 103 | 3 Strokes

This is a little child with his arms wide and his mouth open crying for his mommy.

On: シ
Kun: こ

Meaning: child

Stroke Order:

子 フ 了 子

Examples:

こども
子供 children; child

おとこ こ
男 の子 a boy [man's child = boy]

か し
お菓子 candy; sweets

こねこ
子猫 kitten [child cat]

こ ど も　　す
子供が好きです。
I like children.

Chapter Three: Kanji 21-30
JLPT N5: 21 / 103 | 4 Strokes

On: ニチ

Kun: ひ

Meaning: sun; day

The usual word for sun is 太陽 *taiyou*.

Stroke Order:

Examples:

ある日 one day (as in: One day, Little Red Riding Hood...)

毎日 everyday

今日 today [irregular pronunciation]

日曜日 Sunday [Notice the two sounds of 日: *nichi* and *bi* (which is *hi* with a sound change)]

毎日、日本語を勉強します。

Everyday, I study Japanese.

JLPT N5: 22 / 103 | 4 Strokes

This is a sun (日) with legs–the moon runs faster around the earth. Therefore it needs legs.

On: ガツ; ゲツ

Kun: つき

Meaning: moon; month

Stroke Order:

月 月 刀 月 月

Examples:

いちがつ
一 月 January [lit. 1st month]

こんげつ
今 月 this month

つき
月 the moon

げつようび
月曜日 Monday [all days of the week end in ようび]

きょう　　　げつようび
今日は月曜日です。

Today is Monday.

JLPT N5: 23 / 103 | 4 Strokes

Think of it as sparks coming from a person.

On: カ

Kun: ひ

Meaning: fire

Stroke Order:

火 火 火 火 火

Examples:

はなび
花火 fireworks [note how the ひ becomes a び]

ひばな
火花 sparks [sometimes you can reverse kanji and get a

different meaning; note here how the はな becomes ばな]

かざん
火山 volcano [lit. fire mountain]

かようび
火曜日 Tuesday

かようび
あしたは火曜日です。

Tomorrow is Tuesday.

JLPT N5: 24 / 103 | 4 Strokes

Squeeze a river (川) and you get water.

On: スイ

Kun: みず

Meaning: water

This kanji as a radical often looks like 氵 and is found with kanji dealing with water.

Stroke Order:

水 亅 水 水 水

Examples:

<ruby>大<rt>おお</rt>水<rt>みず</rt></ruby>
大水 flood [lit. big water]

みずぎ
水着 swimsuit; bathing suit

すいようび
水曜日 Wednesday

みずぎ　も
水着を持っていますか？

Do you have your swimming trunks?

JLPT N5: 25 / 103 | 4 Strokes

This is a tree with two low hanging branches.

On: モク; ボク

Kun: き

Meaning: tree

Start with the horizontal line, then vertical. The left and right slanted strokes are last.

Stroke Order:

Examples:

きのぼ
木登り tree climbing

まつ き
松の木 pine tree

もくようび
木曜日 Thursday

こうえん まつの き
公園に松ノ木があります。

There is a pine tree at the park.

38

JLPT N5: 26 / 103 | 8 Strokes

Think of gold being buried deep within a hill

On: キン; コン
Kun: かね

Meaning: gold; money

Usually "*kin*" deals with gold and "*kane*" means money in general.

Stroke Order:

金 ノ 스 스 宇 宇 金 金 金 金

Examples:

かね
お金 money

しょうきん
賞 金 prize money

きんようび
金曜日 Friday

かね か
お金貸してくれる？

Will you loan me some money?

JLPT N5: 27 / 103 | 3 Strokes

It's a **cross** in the **ground**

On: ド; ト
Kun: つち

Meaning: earth; ground; soil

Don't confuse this with "gentleman" 士. The **earth is wider than the cross** for this kanji.

Stroke Order:

Examples:

ねんど
粘土 clay

とち
土地 ground; area; soil

どようび
土曜日 Saturday

とちをうる。
土地を売る。

To sell land.

JLPT N5: 28 / 103 | 5 Strokes

Just as the kanji is made from 木, books are from trees.

On:
Kun: ほん

Meaning: book; counter for long, slender objects

In Japan, you will often see large signs with just this kanji to indicate a bookstore.

Stroke Order:

本 一 十 オ 木 本

Examples:

にほん
日本 Japan

えほん
絵本 a picture book (for children)

ほん
本 a book

ほんや
本屋 bookstore

ほんや
本屋はどこですか？

Where is a bookstore?

JLPT N5: 29 / 103 | 6 Strokes

This is a picture of a person (left) resting against a tree.

On: キュウ
Kun: やす・む

Meaning: rest; vacation

As suggested above, the left part (⼈) is actually "person" (人)

Stroke Order:

休 休 休 仆 什 休 休

Examples:

夏休み summer vacation

昼休み lunch break

お休みなさい Good night!

休んだほうがいい。

We had better rest.

JLPT N5: 30 / 103 | 14 Strokes

語

On: ゴ

Kun: かた・る

Meaning: word; speech; language

It may help to break this down. 言 to speak; 五 the number 5; and the bottom is (口) which means mouth.

Stroke Order:

語 ゛ ー ゠ ゠ ゠ ゠ 言
言 訂 語 語 語 語 語

Examples:

ものがたり
物 語　a story; tale; legend

こくご
国語　national language (in Japan, Japanese)

にほんご
日本語ができます。

I can speak Japanese.

[Note: the できます merely shows ability, so this could mean "I can speak" or "I can understand" or "I can read".]

Chapter Four: Kanji 31-40
This year, study kanji!
JLPT N5: 31 / 103 | 6 Strokes

On: ネン
Kun: とし

Meaning: year

Stroke Order:

年 年 年 年 年 年 年

Examples:

<ruby>一<rt>いち</rt></ruby><ruby>年<rt>ねん</rt></ruby>　one year

<ruby>二<rt>に</rt></ruby><ruby>年<rt>ねん</rt></ruby><ruby>前<rt>まえ</rt></ruby>　two years ago

<ruby>去<rt>きょ</rt></ruby><ruby>年<rt>ねん</rt></ruby>　last year

<ruby>今<rt>こ</rt></ruby><ruby>年<rt>とし</rt></ruby>３０<ruby>歳<rt>さい</rt></ruby>になりました。

I became thirty this year.

[Note: "this year" is "*kotoshi*" not "*kontoshi*".]

44

JLPT N5: 32 / 103 | 4 Strokes

Be careful to not confuse this one with 牛 (cow) .

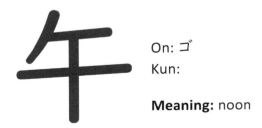

On: ゴ
Kun:

Meaning: noon

This also looks like the previous kanji, year 年 (#31).

Stroke Order:

午 ノ ヶ 午 午

Examples:

<ruby>午<rt>ご</rt></ruby><ruby>後<rt>ご</rt></ruby> afternoon (PM)

<ruby>午<rt>ご</rt></ruby><ruby>前<rt>ぜん</rt></ruby> morning (AM)

<ruby>午<rt>ご</rt></ruby><ruby>後<rt>ご</rt></ruby><ruby>二<rt>に</rt></ruby><ruby>時<rt>じ</rt></ruby> 2 PM

<ruby>午<rt>ご</rt></ruby><ruby>後<rt>ご</rt></ruby>の<ruby>昼<rt>ひる</rt></ruby><ruby>寝<rt>ね</rt></ruby>

Afternoon nap

JLPT N5: 33 / 103 | 9 Strokes

Remember: there is a month in there.

On: ゼン
Kun: まえ

Meaning: before; in front of; previous

This versatile word is used with time and space. [before (time) and in front of (space)]

Stroke Order:

Examples:

<ruby>名<rt>な</rt></ruby><ruby>前<rt>まえ</rt></ruby> name

<ruby>前<rt>まえ</rt></ruby><ruby>書<rt>が</rt></ruby>き preface [lit. before the writing]

<ruby>二<rt>に</rt></ruby><ruby>年<rt>ねん</rt></ruby><ruby>前<rt>まえ</rt></ruby> two years ago

お<ruby>名<rt>な</rt></ruby><ruby>前<rt>まえ</rt></ruby>は<ruby>何<rt>なん</rt></ruby>ですか？

What is your name?

JLPT N5: 34 / 103 | 9 Strokes

When you are "behind" (in space) you are "after" (in time) something or someone.

On: ゴ; コウ
Kun: うし・ろ; のち

Meaning: behind; after

Stroke Order:

後 後 後 後 後 後 後 後 後 後

Examples:

さいご
最後 the last; the end; conclusion

うし
後ろ behind

あとが
後書き postscript; afterword [lit. after the writing]

うし   み
後ろを見て。

Look behind (you).

JLPT N5: 35 / 103 | 10 Strokes

The sun is very important in telling time: 日

時

On: ジ
Kun: とき

Meaning: time

sun 日 + temple 寺

Stroke Order:

時 時 丨 冂 冂 日 日 旪 旪 時 時 時 時

Examples:

じかん
時間 time

ときどき
時々 sometimes [the 々 character means to repeat]

えどじだい
江戸時代 the Edo Period

なんじ
何時ですか？

What time is it?

JLPT N5: 36 / 103 | 12 Strokes

The 門 is the kanji that means "gate." So, in the **interval** of the **gate** there is a **sun**.

On: カン; ケン
Kun: あいだ; ま

Meaning: interval; space; room

Similar kanji are 門 gate and 聞 to hear.

Stroke Order:

丨 冂 冂 冃 冃 門 門 門 問 問 問 間

Examples:

<ruby>時間<rt>じかん</rt></ruby> time
時間 time

昼間 daytime
<ruby>昼間<rt>ひるま</rt></ruby> daytime

居間 living room
<ruby>居間<rt>いま</rt></ruby> living room

時間がありますか？
<ruby>時間<rt>じかん</rt></ruby>がありますか？

Do you have some spare time?

JLPT N5: 37 / 103 | 6 Strokes

On:
Kun: まい

Meaning: every~

Do you see mother? 母 [#15]

Stroke Order:

毎 毎 毎 毎 毎 毎 毎

Examples:

まいにち
毎日　everyday

まいあさ
毎朝　every morning

まいしゅう
毎週　every week

まいにち　に ほ ん ご　べんきょう
毎日、日本語を勉強します。

I study Japanese everyday.

JLPT N5: 38 / 103 | 6 Strokes

It has two legs so it always walks ahead.

先

On: セン
Kun: さき

Meaning: previous; ahead

This word is used for space and time.

Stroke Order:

先 先 先 先 先 先 先

Examples:

<ruby>先<rt>せん</rt></ruby><ruby>生<rt>せい</rt></ruby> teacher

<ruby>先<rt>せん</rt></ruby><ruby>日<rt>じつ</rt></ruby> the other day

どうぞ、お<ruby>先<rt>さき</rt></ruby>に。

Please go first.

JLPT N5: 39 / 103 | 4 Strokes

It looks like someone with a hat is eating with his mouth wide open **now**.

On: コン; キン
Kun: いま

Meaning: now; the present

Stroke Order:

Examples:

こんげつ
今月　this month

こんばん
今晩は　good night [lit. as for this night]

こんど
今度　next time [you would think this means this time!]

ことし　はたち
今年で二十歳になりました。

I became twenty this year.
[Note: "this year" is "*kotoshi*" not "*kontoshi*"]

JLPT N5: 40 / 103 | 6 Strokes

On: カ
Kun: なに; なん

Meaning: what

This is often used with other kanji to show uncertainty.

Stroke Order:

何ノ 亻 亻 仃 仃 何 何

Examples:

なんにん
何人 How many people?

なに
何か something

なに
何？ What?

なんじ
何時ですか？
What time is it?

Chapter Five: Kanji 41-50
The shorter bar is **ABOVE** the longer bar
JLPT N5: 41 / 103 | 3 Strokes

上

On: ジョウ

Kun: うえ; あ・げる; のぼ・る

Meaning: up; to raise up

Don't be shocked at the number of pronunciations (actually there are more!). The best one to remember is うえ.

Stroke Order:

上 丨 卜 上

Examples:

つくえ　うえ
机 の上　on (the) desk [lit. desk's above]

じょうず
上手　to be good at something [lit upper hand]

としうえ
年上　older; old (in years)

うえ　み
上を見てください。

Please look up.

JLPT N5: 42 / 103 | 3 Strokes

The shorter bar is **BELOW** the longer bar

On: カ; ゲ
Kun: した

Meaning: below; under; down

This one also has several more readings, but した is the most useful for now.

Stroke Order:

Examples:

くつした
靴下　socks [lit. shoes under]

ち か
地下　underground; basement

としした
年下　junior; younger; young

くるま　　した　　ねこ
車 の下に猫がいます。

There is a cat under the car.

JLPT N5: 43 / 103 | 5 Strokes

左

On: サ
Kun: ひだり

Meaning: left

Left (左) and right (右) are very similar. Left has a
capital I and right has a mouth.

Stroke Order:

左 左 ナ 左 左 左

Examples:

左手 left hand

左足 left leg

机 の 左 to the left of the desk

左 にあります。

It is on the left.

JLPT N5: 44 / 103 | 5 Strokes

On: ユウ

Kun: みぎ

Meaning: right

Left (左) and right (右) are very similar. Left has a capital I and right has a mouth.

Stroke Order:

右 ノ ナ 右 右 右

Examples:

右目 right eye

右ページ right page (of a book)

右手 right hand

右に曲がります。

I'm turning to the right.
(in a car, for example)

JLPT N5: 45 / 103 | 8 Strokes

In order to look at the **sun** from behind a **tree**, you must be facing **east**.

On: トウ

Kun: ひがし

Meaning: east

A **sun** [日] character behind a **tree** [木].

Stroke Order:

東 東 東 東 東 東 東 東 東

Examples:

ちゅうとう
中 東 the Middle East

ひがし
東 アジア East Asia

とうきょう
東 京 Tokyo

とうきょう　　　す
東 京 に住んでいます。

I live in Tokyo.

JLPT N5: 46 / 103 | 6 Strokes

"Go west!" said the mouth with legs dangling inside.

On: セイ; サイ
Kun: にし

Meaning: west

It would be helpful to spend some time learning the directions well as they can be confusing.

Stroke Order:

Examples:

にしぐち
西口 west entrance

かんさい
関西 Osaka and surrounding area; Kansai

たいせいよう
大西洋 the Atlantic

にし
西はどっち？

Which way is west?

JLPT N5: 47 / 103 | 9 Strokes

Remember: there is money (¥ *yen*) in the **south.**

On: ナン

Kun: みなみ

Meaning: south

Stroke Order:

南 南 南 南 南 南 南 南 南

Examples:

とうなん
東南アジア Southeast Asia

なんきょく
南極 the South Pole; Antarctic

なんべい
南米 South America

みなみ　うみ
南に海があります。

Down south, there is an ocean.

JLPT N5: 48 / 103 | 5 Strokes

It looks **like two people sitting** with their back against the **north pole**.

On: ホク
Kun: きた

Meaning: north

Stroke Order:

北 北 北 北 北 北

Examples:

<ruby>北海道<rt>ほっかいどう</rt></ruby>
北海道 Hokkaido (most northern part of Japan)

きた
北アメリカ North America

べきん
北京 Beijing (China)

なんぼくせんそう
南北戦争 the (US) Civil War

ほっかいどう　　い
北海道へ行ったことがありますか？

Have you ever been to Hokkaido?

JLPT N5: 49 / 103 | 5 Strokes

Looks like an **axe** cutting a tree down **outside**.

On: ガイ; ゲ
Kun: ほか; そと

Meaning: outside; foreign; other

"Foreigner" is often abbreviated as *gaijin* but this can be considered an insult. 外国人 is better.

Stroke Order:

外 ク ク タ 外 外

Examples:

外国人 foreigner

外国語 foreign language

外で遊ぼう。

Let's play outside.

JLPT N5: 50 / 103 | 6 Strokes

On: メイ; ミョウ
Kun: な

Meaning: fame; famous; name

Stroke Order:

名 ノ ク タ タ 名 名

Examples:

なまえ
名前 name

ゆうめい
有名 famous

ひらがな
平仮名 Hiragana [the Japanese writing system]

わたし　　なまえ
私 の名前は〜です。

My name is...

Chapter Six: Kanji 51-60
JLPT N5: 51 / 103 | 10 Strokes

On: コウ

Kun: たか・い

Meaning: high; tall; costly

Think of this as a picture of a **tall** and **costly** Japanese **building**

Stroke Order:

高 高 高 高 高 高 高 高 高 高 高

Examples:

^{さいこう}
最高 the highest; the best; supreme [not to be confused with "psycho"]

^{こうこうせい}
高校生 a high school student

^{たか}
高いビル a tall building

^{やさい}^{たか}
野菜が高いです。

The vegetables are expensive.

JLPT N5: 52 / 103 | 3 Strokes

On: しょう
Kun: ちい・さい；こ；お

Meaning: small; little

Only three **small** strokes make up this little kanji.

Stroke Order:

小 亅 小 小

Examples:

しょうがっこう
小学校 elementary school

ちい　　いえ
小さい家 a small house

しょうせつ
小説 a novel, a story (fiction)

ちい　　くるま
小さい車 がほしい。

I want a small car.

JLPT N5: 53 / 103 | 4 Strokes

On: チュウ

Kun: なか

Meaning: middle; center; within; inside

It's a line **inside** a box!

Stroke Order:

中 中 中 中 中

Examples:

いちにちじゅう
一 日 中 all day long (sound changes from ちゅう to じゅう)

いえ　なか
家の中 inside the house

べんきょうちゅう
勉 強 中 while studying; in the midst of studying

かれ　ゆき　なか　ある
彼は雪の中を歩きました。

He was walking through the snow.

JLPT N5: 54 / 103 | 3 Strokes

On: ダイ; タイ
Kun: おお・きい

Meaning: big; large

This is a **big** person (人) with his **great** arms spread wide.

Stroke Order:

大 一 ナ 大

Examples:

だいがく
大学 university, college

おお こころ
大きい 心 a big heart

だいかい
大会 big meet; convention; rally

あたま おお
あなたの 頭 は大きいです。

Your head is big.

JLPT N5: 55 / 103 | 8 Strokes

On: チョウ

Kun: なが・い

Meaning: long; (*chou*— head of an organization; leader)

There are several **long** strokes to make this kanji.

Stroke Order:

長 長 長 長 長 長 長 長 長

Examples:

こうちょうせんせい
校 長 先 生　principal (of school)

しゃちょう
社 長　a company president

なが　みち
長い道　a long road

アマゾン川は世界一長い川です。

The Amazon is the longest river in the world.

JLPT N5: 56 / 103 | 5 Strokes

On: ハン
Kun:

Meaning: half

The two top half lines were cut in **half.**

Stroke Order:

半 ㇏ ㇐ 半 ㇐ 半

Examples:

はんつき
半月 a half moon

はんとう
半島 peninsula [lit. half island]

はんぶん お
やっと半分終わった。

Finally, I'm half-way finished.

JLPT N5: 57 / 103 | 4 Strokes

On: ふん; ぶん
Kun: わ・ける

Meaning: part; portion

The bottom part is a sword (刀) and think of the sword dividing the top **part** into two **parts**.

Stroke Order:

Examples:

はんぶん
半分 half

ぶぶん
部分 a part

きぶん
気分 feeling; mood

わ
分かりました I understand

はい、分かります。

Yes, I understand.

JLPT N5: 58 / 103 | 8 Strokes

On: ガク
Kun: まな・ぶ

Meaning: learning; study

The bottom is a child (子) and think of the top as his brain waves **learning.**

Stroke Order:

Examples:

<ruby>科<rt>か</rt></ruby><ruby>学<rt>がく</rt></ruby> science

<ruby>中<rt>ちゅう</rt></ruby><ruby>学<rt>がっ</rt></ruby><ruby>校<rt>こう</rt></ruby> middle school; JHS

<ruby>数<rt>すう</rt></ruby><ruby>学<rt>がく</rt></ruby> math; arithmetic

<ruby>数<rt>すう</rt></ruby><ruby>学<rt>がく</rt></ruby>できません。

I can't do math.

JLPT N5: 59 / 103 | 10 Strokes

On: コウ
Kun:

Meaning: school

Many **school** buildings are made of trees 木.

Stroke Order:

校校校校校校校校校校校

Examples:

がっこう
学校 school

こうこう
高校 senior high school

こうない
校内 within the school; on school grounds

あなたの学校はどこですか？
がっこう

Where is your school?

72

JLPT N5: 60 / 103 | 5 Strokes

On: セイ; ショウ
Kun: う・む; い・きる

Meaning: birth; life; to give birth; to live

Stroke Order:

生 ノ ト 牛 牛 生

Examples:

がくせい
学生 a student

いっしょう
一 生 all life; a lifetime

じんせい
人生 life (human)

せんせい
先生 teacher; master; doctor...

せんせい　　　　ひと
先生はあの人です。

The teacher is that person over there.

Chapter Seven: Kanji 61-70
JLPT N5: 61 / 103 | 3 Strokes

On: サン

Kun: やま

Meaning: mountain

Think of it as a range of three **mountains**, the tallest being in the center.

Stroke Order:

Examples:

かざん
火山 a volcano [lit. fire mountain]

ふじさん
富士山 Mt. fuji [contrary to popular belief, the *"san"* in

"fujisan" is not "Mr." It means, rather, "mountain."]

やま
ごみの山 a mountain of garbage

やま
山 a mountain

ふじさん　　のぼ
富士山に登ったことがありますか？

Have you climbed Mt. Fuji before?

74

JLPT N5: 62 / 103 | 3 Strokes

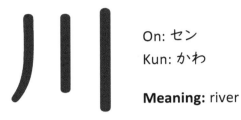

On: セン
Kun: かわ

Meaning: river

This is a picture of water flowing down a stream.

Stroke Order:

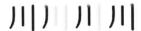

Examples:

かわ
川 a river

いしかわけん
石川県 Ishikawa prefecture (on Honshu)

おがわ
小川 a stream [lit. small river]

いえ　　　　　　かわ
家のうしろに川があります。

There is a river behind the house.

JLPT N5: 63 / 103 | 5 Strokes

On: ハク; ビャク

Kun: しろ

Meaning: white

Don't confuse this with 自 which means "self"—**white has one line** and 自 has two lines.

Stroke Order:

白 白 白 白 白

Examples:

しろ
白い the color white

しろ
白あり termite [lit. white ant]

はくちょう
白鳥 swan [lit. white bird]

しろ ねこ か
白い猫を飼っています。

I have a white cat.

JLPT N5: 64 / 103 | 4 Strokes

On: テン
Kun: あま; あめ

Meaning: heaven; sky

Heaven is BIGGER than the kanji for big (大). Therefore, there is a line above it.

Stroke Order:

天 天 天 天 天

Examples:

てんじょう
天井   ceiling

てんき
天気 weather

てんごく
天国   heaven; paradise

てんさい
天才 genius

てんきよほう
天気予報はどう？

How's the weather forecast looking?

JLPT N5: 65 / 103 | 8 Strokes

On: ウ
Kun: あめ; あま

Meaning: rain

Think of the top as the sky opening to release the rain.

Stroke Order:

Examples:

<ruby>雨<rt>あめ</rt></ruby> rain

<ruby>雨水<rt>あまみず</rt></ruby> rain water

<ruby>大雨<rt>おおあめ</rt></ruby> heavy rain

<ruby>最低<rt>さいてい</rt></ruby>!また<ruby>雨<rt>あめ</rt></ruby>か。

It's the pits... Rain again.

JLPT N5: 66 / 103 | 13 Strokes

On: デン

Kun:

Meaning: electricity; electric powered

Notice the top part is rain, so think of electric lightning.

Stroke Order:

電電電電電電電電
電電霄霄雷電

Examples:

でんしゃ
電車 (electric) train

でんち
電池 a battery

でんわ
電話 a telephone

でんき
電気 electricity; light (from light bulb...)

あおき　　　　でんわ
青木さんに電話してください。

Please call Mr. Aoki.

JLPT N5: 67 / 103 | 6 Strokes

On: キ; ケ

Kun:

Meaning: spirit; mind; power; energy; intention

This is a fun kanji to draw. Sometimes the best way to learn to read a kanji is by drawing it many times.

Stroke Order:

気 気 気 気 気 気 気

Examples:

<ruby>空気<rt>くうき</rt></ruby> air; atmosphere

<ruby>元気<rt>げんき</rt></ruby> genki; healthy; full of spirit

<ruby>電気<rt>でんき</rt></ruby> electricity; light (from light bulb...)

<ruby>人気<rt>にんき</rt></ruby> popular

あまり<ruby>元気<rt>げんき</rt></ruby>じゃないです。

I'm not feeling very well.

JLPT N5: 68 / 103 | 7 Strokes

On: シャ
Kun: くるま

Meaning: car; vehicle

Using your imagination (to the limits of your ability), you may see a **car** with four wheels.

Stroke Order:

車 車 車 車 車 車 車 車

Examples:

でんしゃ
電車 train

じてんしゃ
自転車 bicycle

きゅうきゅうしゃ
救 急 車 ambulance

くるま　　しず
この 車 は静かです。

This car is quiet.

JLPT N5: 69 / 103 | 8 Strokes

This is a combination of kuchi (口) [mouth] and tama (玉) [ball]. You can also think of something being contained by boundaries (countries are lands separated by boundaries).

On: コク
Kun: くに

Meaning: country; nation

Stroke Order:

Examples:

かんこく
韓国 Korea

がいこく
外国 foreign country

ちゅうごく
中国 China

あの国<ruby>国<rt>くに</rt></ruby>は、なぜ貧<ruby><rt>まず</rt></ruby>しいのか？

I wonder why that country is poor?

JLPT N5: 70 / 103 | 4 Strokes

This is often used instead of the Yen symbol ¥

On: エン
Kun: まる・い

Meaning: circle; yen (money)

It seems **money** has **legs** and is always **leaving**.

Stroke Order:

Examples:

せんえん
千円 1000 yen

えんだか
円高 a high yen rate

まる
円をかく draw a circle

せんえん
千円がありますか？

Do you have a thousand yen?

Chapter Eight: Kanji 71-80

Most kanji are made of parts. The left side means "a word" and the right side means "tongue."

JLPT N5: 71 / 103 | 13 Strokes

話

On: ワ

Kun: はなし; はな・す

Meaning: a talk; a topic; a story

Stroke Order:

話 話 話 話 言 言 言 言 話 話 話 話 話

Examples:

えいかいわ
英会話 English conversation (class)

むかしばなし
昔 話   an old tale, legend [note how the "*hanashi*"

becomes "*banashi*"

しゅわ
手話 sign language [lit. hand talk]

きのうの 話 聞いた?

Did you hear yesterday's speech?

JLPT N5: 72 / 103 | 14 Strokes

This is a combination of gate (門) and ear (耳). People go to the gate to hear news.

On: ブン
Kun: き・く

Meaning: to hear; to listen; ask

Stroke Order:

｜ ｢ ｢ ｢ ｢ 門 門 門 門 門 門 門 聞 聞

Examples:

しんぶん
新 聞 newspaper

き　　　くだ
聞いて下さい please listen

あさひしんぶん
朝日新 聞 the Asahi newspaper

はなし き
きのうの 話 聞いた?

Did you hear yesterday's speech?

JLPT N5: 73 / 103 | 9 Strokes

It looks like a **person reclining** under his **roof eating** something.

On: じき；しょく
Kun: く・う；た・べる

Meaning: food; to eat; relating to food

Think of eating good (良) food.

Stroke Order:

Examples:

しょくじ
食事　a meal

た　もの
食べ物　food; something to eat

た
食べにくい　difficult to eat

た
もう食べた？

Did you eat already?

JLPT N5: 74 / 103 | 14 Strokes

The left part means "a word" and the right part means "to sell." So a **book** is a **bought word**.

On: どく
Kun: よ・む

Meaning: to read

Stroke Order:

読 読 読 読 読 読 読 読
読 読 読 読 読 読 読

Examples:

よ
読みやすい easy to read

どくしょ
読書 reading

よ
読んで下さい。

Please read.

JLPT N5: 75 / 103 | 7 Strokes

This is one of the very few irregular verbs: くる becomes きます in the -masu form.

On: ライ
Kun: く・る

Meaning: to come

Stroke Order:

来 来 来 来 来 来 来 来

Examples:

みらい
未来 the future [lit. not yet come]
らいげつ
来月 next month
てき
出来る able to do something; ready for

あとで来る？

Will you come later?

JLPT N5: 76 / 103 | 10 Strokes

On: ショ
Kun: か・く

Meaning: book; document; to write

Also remember there is a **sun** at the **bottom**; after all, **you must have light to read!**

Stroke Order:

Examples:

としょかん
図書館 library

せいしょ
聖書 the Bible [lit. holy book]

じしょ
辞書 dictionary

としょかん
図書館はどこですか？

Where is the library?

JLPT N5: 77 / 103 | 7 Strokes

The top part is 目 (eye) and think of the bottom as legs.
Therefore actively using your eyes means to see.

On: ケン
Kun: み・る; み・せる

Meaning: *to see; to show*

Stroke Order:

見 見 冂 冃 月 目 見 見

Examples:

み
見せて show me!

はなみ
花見 flower viewing; watching cherry blossoms in April

み
見える be able to see; visible

ほし　　　み
あの星が見えますか？

Can you see that star?

JLPT N5: 78 / 103 | 6 Strokes

It looks like a side view of a dog (with no tail) ready **to go**.

行

On: ギョウ；コウ
Kun: い・く

Meaning: to go

Stroke Order:

行 行 行 行 行 行 行

Examples:

<ruby>銀行<rt>ぎんこう</rt></ruby> bank

<ruby>旅行<rt>りょこう</rt></ruby> a trip; travel

<ruby>行<rt>い</rt></ruby>きましょう。

Let's go.

JLPT N5: 79 / 103 | 5 Strokes

This looks like a **mountain 山 on a mountain**—it actually is not—but think of going out to the mountains.

On: シュツ
Kun: だ・す；で・る

Meaning: to go out; leave

Stroke Order:

出 丨 十 屮 出 出

Examples:

<ruby>出口<rt>てぐち</rt></ruby>　exit

<ruby>出発<rt>しゅっぱつ</rt></ruby>　to go; departure

<ruby>思<rt>おも</rt></ruby>い<ruby>出<rt>だ</rt></ruby>す　to remember; to recollect

<ruby>出口<rt>てぐち</rt></ruby>はどこですか？

Where is the exit?

JLPT N5: 80 / 103 | 2 Strokes

It looks very much like the kanji for a person (人) but with a little hat on.

On: ニュウ
Kun: い・る； はい・る

Meaning: to enter; to go in; insert

Stroke Order:

Examples:

なかい
中入り intermission (of a play)

いりぐち
入口 an entrance

て　はい
手に入る to obtain; to get your hands on..

いりぐち
この入口はわかりにくいです。

This entrance isn't easy to find.

Chapter Nine: Kanji 81-90

Think of this kanji as a person sitting at a desk under a roof. Most **meetings** take place in a **house** with **desks**.

On: カイ

Kun: あ・う

Meaning: to meet; meeting

Stroke Order:

Examples:

<ruby>えいかいわ</ruby>
英会話 English conversation [*kaiwa* by itself means any conversation]

<ruby>かいぎ</ruby>
会議 meeting; conference

<ruby>きょうかい</ruby>
教 会 church

<ruby>いま</ruby>　<ruby>かいぎ</ruby>
今から会議をはじめる。

The meeting will begin now.

JLPT N5: 82 / 103 | 10 Strokes

Paper is made up of tiny threads 糸 or fibers.

On: シ
Kun: かみ

Meaning: paper

Stroke Order:

く 幺 幺 糸 糸 糸 糸 糸 紙 紙 紙

Examples:

てがみ
手紙 letter (postal)

わし
和紙 Japanese style paper

お　がみ
折り紙 origami

かみぶくろ
紙 袋をいただけますか。

May I have a paper bag?

JLPT N5: 83 / 103 | 7 Strokes

Words coming out of a mouth 口.

On: ゲン　ゴン
Kun: い.う　こと

Meaning: say; speech

Stroke Order:

言 言 言 言 言 言 言 言

Examples:

ことば
言葉 language; dialect; word; phrase; speech

むごん
無言 silence

ほうげん
方言 dialect

むし　なん　い
この虫は何と言いますか？

What do you call this insect?

JLPT N5: 84 / 103 | 12 Strokes

Answer with your mouth 口 and a bamboo stick 竹.

答

On: トウ
Kun: こた.える　こた.え

Meaning: solution; answer

Stroke Order:

答 答 答 答 答 答 答
竺 竺 答 答 答 答

Examples:

かいとう
解答 answer; solution (to a problem or question)

じもんじとう
自問自答 answering one's own question; soliloquizing;

wondering to oneself

こた　　　　まちが
その答えは間違っている。

That answer is incorrect.

JLPT N5: 85 / 103 | 9 Strokes

A thousand 千 people 人 ride a 9 stroke car.

On: ジョウ　ショウ
Kun: の.る　-の.り　の.せる

Meaning: ride; board

Stroke Order:

乗 乗 乗 乗 乗 乗 乗 乗 乗

Examples:

の　　ば
乗り場 a place for boarding vehicles

の　　もの
乗り物 vehicle

の　　こ
乗り越える to overcome; to climb over

の　　ば
バスの乗り場はどこですか？

Where is the bus boarding area?

JLPT N5: 86 / 103 | 12 Strokes

Keep an eye 目 open for his arrival.

On: チャク　ジャク
Kun: き.る　-ぎ　き.せる　-
き.せ　つ.く　つ.ける

Meaning: don; wear; arrive

Stroke Order:

着着着着着着着
着着着着着着

Examples:

とうちゃく
到着 arrival

きもの
着物 kimono; clothing

したぎ
下着 underwear

あたら　　みずぎ　か
新しい水着を買いました。

I bought new swimwear.

JLPT N5: 87 / 103 | 14 Strokes

There are horses 馬 at the station.

On: エキ
Kun:

Meaning: station

Stroke Order:

駅 駅 駅 駅 駅 馬 馬 馬
馬 馬 駅 駅 駅 駅 駅

Examples:

えきまえ
駅 前 front of station (where many shops are)

えきちょう
駅 長 station master

むじんえき
無人駅 unstaffed train station

れっしゃ　おおさかえき　で
列車は大阪駅を出た。

The train left for Osaka station.

JLPT N5: 88 / 103 | 8 Strokes

There are clothes 衣 on the schedule.

On: ヒョウ
Kun: おもて　-おもて　あら
わ.す　あらわ.れる　あら.
わす

Meaning: surface; table;
chart; diagram

Stroke Order:

表　一　十　耂　耂　表　表　表　表

Examples:

だいひょう
代 表　representative; delegation

はっぴょう
発 表　announcement

ひょうじょう
表 情　facial expression

おもて　うら
表 か裏か？

Heads or tails?

JLPT N5: 89 / 103 | 7 Strokes

Humans 人 create. The radical to the left イ represents
人.

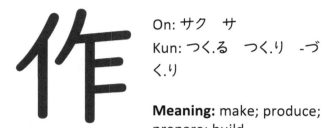

On: サク　サ
Kun: つく.る　つく.り　-づ
く.り

Meaning: make; produce;
prepare; build

Stroke Order:

作 イ イ 作 作 作 作

Examples:

さっか
作家 author; novelist; writer
さくせん
作戦 tactics; strategy; military operations
てづく
手作り handmade; homegrown; hand-crafted

ぎゅうにゅう　　つく
チーズは 牛 乳 で作る。

Cheese is made from milk.

JLPT N5: 90 / 103 | 7 Strokes

Looks like someone kneeling *near* a stream.

近

On: キン　コン
Kun: ちか.い

Meaning: near; early

Stroke Order:

近　斤　厂　斤　斤　沂　近　近

Examples:

さいきん
最近 recently; these days; nowadays

きんじょ
近所 neighborhood

ちかみち
近道 shortcut

ちか　　　　ぎんこう
近くに銀行がある。
There is a bank nearby.

Chapter Ten: Kanji 91-103

The town has rice paddys 田.

JLPT N5: 91 / 103 | 7 Strokes

町

On: チョウ

Kun: まち

Meaning: town; village; block

Stroke Order:

町 l 冂 冂 用 田 町 町

Examples:

ちょうみん
町 民 townspeople

となりまち
隣 町 neighboring town

なんてすてきな街なんだ！

まち

What a nice town!

JLPT N5: 92 / 103 | 10 or 11 Strokes

On: シュウ

Kun:

Meaning: week

Depending how you write the radical 辶, this kanji has 10 of 11 strokes

Stroke Order:

週 丿 刀 月 冂 冃 冄
円 周 冏 调 週

Examples:

いっしゅうかん
一 週 間 a span of one week

こんしゅう
今 週 this week

まいしゅう　つ　　　い
毎 週、釣りに行きます。

Every week (I) go fishing.

105

JLPT N5: 93 / 103 | 7 Strokes

People 亻 live near the king 王.

住

On: ジュウ　ヂュウ　チュウ
Kun: す.む　す.まう　-ず.ま
い

Meaning: live; dwell; inhabit

The 亻 radical is a stylized 人 person.

Stroke Order:

住 亻 亻 亻 住 住 住

Examples:

じゅうたく
住 宅　residence; housing; residential building

じゅうみん
住 民　citizens; inhabitants; residents; population

じゅうしょ
住 所　(house) address

いえ　　す　　　せま
この家は、住むには狭すぎる。

This house is too small for (us) to live in.

JLPT N5: 94 / 103 | 8 Strokes

It's wise to shoot arrows 矢 from your mouth 口.

知

On: チ
Kun: し.る　し.らせる

Meaning: know; wisdom

Stroke Order:

知 ⺮ ⺈ ⺌ ⺬ 矢 知 知 知

Examples:

<ruby>知<rt>ち</rt></ruby><ruby>事<rt>じ</rt></ruby> prefectural governer (in Japan)

<ruby>知<rt>ち</rt></ruby><ruby>識<rt>しき</rt></ruby> knowledge; information

<ruby>知<rt>し</rt></ruby>り<ruby>合<rt>あ</rt></ruby>い an acquaintance

<ruby>彼女<rt>かのじょ</rt></ruby>は<ruby>知<rt>し</rt></ruby>らん<ruby>顔<rt>かお</rt></ruby>をした。

She gave off a look of indifference.

[<ruby>知<rt>し</rt></ruby>らん<ruby>顔<rt>かお</rt></ruby> means "unconcerned air," "feigned

ignorance," or "pretending not to recognize someone."]

JLPT N5: 95 / 103 | 6 Strokes

Women 女 *like* children 子.

好

On: コウ
Kun: この.む　す.く　よ.い
い.い

Meaning: fond; pleasing; to like something

Stroke Order:

好 く 女 女 好 好 好

Examples:

だいす
大好き love; live very much

なかよ
仲良く on good terms with; get along with; peacefully

す きら
好き嫌い likes and dislikes; pickiness (usually about food);
choosy

かれ　おんがく　この　　　すば
彼の音楽の好みは素晴らしい。

His tastes in music is superb.

JLPT N5: 96 / 103 | 8 Strokes

My elder sister is a woman 女 who lives in the city 市.

On: シ
Kun: あね

Meaning: older sister

This kanji is made of two parts: 女 (woman) and 市 city or market — an **older sister** goes to the **city**.

Stroke Order:

姉 く 女 女 女 姉 姉 姉 姉

Examples:

^{ねえ}
お姉さん big sister (honorific—changes from *"ane"* to *"onee"*)

^{ねえ}
姉さん girl; older girl

^{しまい}
姉妹 sisters

お姉さんはどこですか？

Where is your older sister?

JLPT N5: 97 / 103 | 7 Strokes

My younger brother has a bow 弓 without arrows.

On: テイ　ダイ　デ

Kun: おとうと

Meaning: younger brother

It is hard to see, but the radical is actually a 弓 bow (bow and arrow).

Stroke Order:

弟 弟 弟 弟 弟 弟 弟 弟

Examples:

きょうだい
兄 弟　siblings; brothers and sisters

で し
弟子 student; apprentice; disciple

おとうと　　　じゅうごさい
弟 は十五歳です。

My kid brother is fifteen.

JLPT N5: 98 / 103 | 9 Strokes

Every 毎 ocean has water 氵 (radical for water).

海

On: カイ

Kun: うみ

Meaning: ocean; sea

Stroke Order:

海 海 海 海 海 海 海 海 海

Examples:

うんかい
雲海 sea of clouds (seen above the clouds from a plane)
ほっかいどう
北海道 Hokkaido (northernmost island of Japan)
にほんかい
日本海 Sea of Japan

うみ　　　　ひろ
海はとても広い。

The sea is very wide.

JLPT N5: 99 / 103 | 6 Strokes

On: アン
Kun: やす・い

Meaning: 1) safe; peaceful; 2) cheap; inexpensive

Remember this kanji has two different meanings: 1) safe and 2) cheap

Stroke Order:

安 安 安 安 安 安 安

Examples:

あんしん
安心 peace of mind

やす
安いもの something cheap

あんぜん
安全 safe, safety

やす
これは安いですね。

Isn't this inexpensive!

JLPT N5: 100 / 103 | 12 Strokes

Buy with seashells 貝.

On: バイ
Kun: か.う

Meaning: buy

Stroke Order:

買買買買買買買
買買買買買買

Examples:

か　もの
買い物 shopping; purchased goods
か　どく
買い得 a bargain; a good buy

かれ　くるま　か
彼は 車 を買いたい。
He wants to buy a car.

JLPT N5: 101 / 103 | 4 Strokes

Cross your legs when you write a sentence.

On: ブン　モン
Kun: ふみ　あや

Meaning: sentence;
literature; style; art

Stroke Order:

Examples:

ぶんぽう
文 法 grammar

ぶんか
文化 culture; civilization

ぶんがく
文 学 literature

に ほ ん ご　　ぶんしょう　　か
日本語の 文 章 を書いてください。

Please write a sentence in Japanese.

JLPT N5: 102 / 103 | 5 Strokes

When you are right, put a hat on and stop 止.

正

On: セイ　ショウ
Kun: ただ.しい　ただ.す
まさ

Meaning: correct; justice; righteous

Stroke Order:

正 正 丁 下 正 正

Examples:

せいぎ
正義 justice; right

しょうがつ
正 月 New Year; New Year's Day; January

せいかい
正解 correct; right answer

ただ
あなたはまったく正しくない。
You are absolutely incorrect.

JLPT N5: 103 / 103 | 18 Strokes

People work and live 住 under the sun 日 during the week.

On: ヨウ
Kun:

Meaning: weekday

Stroke Order:

丨 冂 冃 日 日ユ 日ヨ 日ヨ 日ヨ1 日ヨヨ 日ヨヨ 日ヨヨ
日ヨヨ 日ヨヨ 日ヨヨ 曜 曜 曜 曜

Examples:

かようび
火曜日 Tuesday

なんようび
何曜日 which day

にちようばん
日曜版 Sunday edition (of newspaper)

どようび　よる
土曜日の夜はどうかな？
How about Saturday night?

Congratulations

You've now mastered some of the most essential kanji in Japanese. For additional free resources, visit https://TheJapanesePage.com for articles on kanji, grammar, and vocabulary. Explore our store at https://www.TheJapanShop.com for books and other learning materials. Take advantage of our half-priced bundle on all Japanese Readers and sign up for our newsletter to receive a free eBook.

To download FREE sound files and Anki decks for all the examples found in this book, please enter the address below in a browser on your computer. The filenames correspond to the numbering found in this ebook.

https://japanesereaders.com/1042-2/

Thank you for purchasing and reading this book! To contact the authors, please email us at *help@thejapanshop.com*. See also the wide selection of materials for learning Japanese at *www.TheJapanShop.com* and the free site for learning Japanese at *www.thejapanesepage.com.*